SANDY SILVERTHORNE'S

SURVIVING
When You're
HOME ALONE

How to avoid being grounded for life

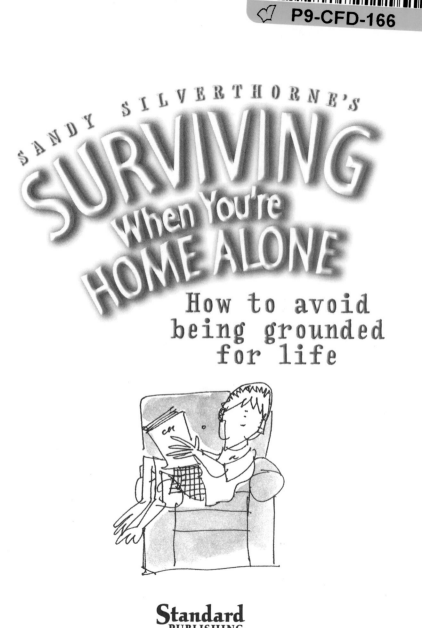

Standard
PUBLISHING

CINCINNATI, OHIO

Project editors: Amy Beveridge and Jennifer Holder.
Cover and interior design: Robert Glover. Typesetting: Peggy Theile.

Scripture taken from the *New King James Version*. Copyright © 1982
by Thomas Nelson, Inc. Used by permission. All rights reserved.

Published in association with the literary agency of Alive Communications,
Inc., 7680 Goddard Street., Suite 200, Colorado Springs, Colorado, 80920.

ISBN 0-7847-1434-7

09 08 07 06 05 04 03   9 8 7 6 5 4 3 2 1

TABLE OF CONTENTS

INTRODUCTION

On my own 4

CHAPTER 1

Realistic expectations—a matter of trust 7

CHAPTER 2

Getting the work done 25

CHAPTER 3

Snacktime! 45

CHAPTER 4

I'm bored! 61

CHAPTER 5

Safety & handling emergencies 75

ON MY OWN

So your parents have decided that you're old enough to stay by yourself until they get home from work. Congratulations! You're growing up and your parents are giving you more responsibility. This is an exciting step for you, but you're going to discover there are some definite challenges to this whole "home alone" deal, too. Don't worry about a thing! This book has been created especially for you.

The following pages are full of great ideas for what to do when you're bored, how to keep safe at home, and even how to deal with your feelings as you start this brand-new routine. And you'll hear from three kids just like you who know all the ropes of being home alone: Eddie, who's been raised by his mom for eleven years, and Kacey and Oliver, whose parents both work full-time. These three really know what's up. So pull up a comfortable chair, grab some cheese snacks, and get ready to ease into this new adventure. You're going to be great!

It was obvious that Michael
and his parents needed to discuss
their expectations for after school. . .

CHAPTER 1:
Realistic expectations
—a matter of trust

WHAT AM I FEELING?

Does the thought of being home alone make you a little nervous? What is it about being on your own that makes you scared or uncomfortable? Are there specific scenarios that worry you? (Some of them will be covered in this rather cool book.)

Even when you're home alone, you're not really alone. There's someone who's always going to be there when you get home—the Lord. He cares about you more than anyone on earth ever could. God wants to use this home-alone time to get closer to you. So let him know what's going on with you. He'll listen—and answer.

WHAT SHOULD I EXPECT FROM MY PARENTS?

Your parents love you and care about you so much. They want you to feel comfortable and safe. This doesn't mean you should go around demanding things or throwing tantrums if you don't get your way. But it does mean you can talk to them about what you feel. Whatever you're feeling, it's important to let your mom or dad know about it. Tell them what they can do to help you be comfortable on your own.

Here's a list of concerns you may want to discuss with your mom and dad.

1. Can they get some snack food for you to eat when you get home?

2. Will they have time to help you with your homework later on?

3. Can you go to a friend's house?

4. Should you check in with a neighbor when you reach your house?

5. Could you call your mom or dad at work when you get home?

Here's a helpful guide to show you how to and how not to share your feelings.

Right

Wrong

As you can see, the girl on the left is expressing herself calmly and respectfully. Her parents will be more inclined to stay and listen to her. But the girl on the right is yelling and screaming so her parents are probably going to leave the room.

WHAT DO THEY EXPECT FROM ME?

OK. Let's get real. You've told your parents how you feel and what you need from them. Now let's see exactly what your parents expect from you. Here are some questions to ask.

1. Do your parents expect you to do some chores when you get home?

2. Are you supposed to start your homework right away or can you loaf around for a while?

3. Do they want you to get dinner ready (that's a long shot) or maybe go to the store or the local fast-food place to pick something up?

4. What are the rules for the TV or the Internet?

Remember the key word in family communication is *respect*. You want your parents to hear you and respect you and your needs, so you need to show them that same respect. If your parents don't agree with you or aren't treating you with respect, just trust God and honor them anyway.

After all, in God's Ten Commandments, number five is "Honor your father and your mother." If God put this in his original "Top Ten" list, then it must be pretty important. As you obey God in this area, he's going to honor your obedience and open up some great opportunities for you.

⟨N⟩ REALITY CHECK

Learning to communicate with your mom, your dad, and even your brothers and sisters is a really important aspect of growing up. Try thinking of your family as your boot camp. As you learn to talk and listen and share what's going on inside of you, God's training you for all the relationships you're going to have in the future.

So now's the time to practice. Learn how to express yourself honestly and kindly. And learn how to listen. Don't be thinking of the next thing you're going to say while someone else is talking. Really listen to what your family is saying. That's the beginning of real communication.

BOTTOM LINE

In Paul's letter to the Ephesians he says we're to "speak the truth in love" (4:15). That means being honest and open, but always in the context of love and compassion. Try communicating with your family this way. It really works.

Here's how I feel about being home alone . . .

If I could change one thing about this situation
it would be . . .

Here are some ways my parents can help me feel
comfortable with staying home alone . . .

You
Are
Here

Here is a list of things my parents expect me
to do while I'm home alone . . .

GOOD CHOICES

God is faithful, who will not allow you to be tempted beyond what you are able. 1 Corinthians 10:13

One of the cool things about getting older is people—your parents especially—start to trust you with more and more responsibility. Taking good care of yourself (and the house!) when you're home alone is a great way to show your parents that you can be trusted.

In order to live up to your parents' trust, you're going to need something called *integrity*. Someone who has integrity does the right thing even when nobody's looking. Someone with integrity does the right thing just because it's right—and that pleases God.

Believe it or not, having integrity can be harder than it may seem. There's a funny thing that happens after you've been alone for a while. A little voice sneaks in and whispers in your ear, "Did you notice that nobody's around? In fact, no one in the whole world knows where you are or what you're doing right now. You could do anything you want, including bad stuff, and no one would ever know."

That's the voice of the tempter encouraging you to take advantage of your home-alone freedom. You may be tempted to do something as simple as neglecting your chores, skipping your homework, or leaving the house when you're supposed to stay put. Or you may be facing the temptation to watch something you know you're not supposed to watch, or worse.

It doesn't matter if you're young or old, girl or boy, the tempting voice may say things like, "Come on, it's not going to hurt anything."

Here's a list of things kids who are home alone may be tempted to do.

1. Skip their chores.
2. Blow off their homework.
3. Torture their brother or sister.
4. Get on the Internet and check out some adult sites.
5. Watch TV shows they know aren't good for them.
6. Get some alcohol or drugs and get high.
7. Have kids over that their parents wouldn't approve of.
8. Smoke.
9. All of the above.

WHAT AM I GOING TO DO?

So what are you going to do? Don't panic because there is a way to face temptation and still come out alive. Just ask Oliver "Flav" Flavinoid. When all the other kids were playing or going to the beach or camping last summer, Oliver was writing a research paper about temptation-fighting strategies for young people. Of course he couldn't wait to share his findings with us.

How to Fight Temptation
by Oliver Flavinoid

As I studied a variety of young people in my research for this project (OK, so it was just my sister and Eddie), I found that subjects who were proactive had more success facing that little tempter voice. When I say proactive I mean . . . um . . . get him before he gets you.

In other words, think of a strategy ahead of time. Don't wait until you're in the middle of a tempting situation to figure out what you're going to do. Do it now. Below, I've jotted down a couple of things that may come up when you're home alone. Take a minute and write down what you'd like to do in each case.

Here's what I mean.

1. Your parents asked you to do some chores, but, you're not in the mood.
   What will you do?

2. You've got some homework assignments to do but couldn't care less about doing them.
   What will you do?

3. You're home alone and suddenly want to watch some trashy TV.
   What will you do?

4. You're on the Internet and you get the urge to check out some bad stuff.
   What will you do?

5. You're on the Internet and some bad stuff finds you. That is, you get an e-mail or message that you know will connect you to an adult site.
   What will you do?

6. A friend comes over with a six pack of beer and wants to drink it with you.
   What will you do?

CHOICE AND CONSEQUENCE

Not to be a total downer here, but every choice you make has some consequences. Some of them are even worse than getting grounded!

If you don't think it's a big deal to surf through some questionable stuff on the Internet, think about this. The images in some of that bad stuff stays in your head for a long time. Do you really want that junk floating around in your head years from now?

Some of the sexual stuff on the Internet is designed to hook you. It seems pretty harmless at first, but pretty soon you're thinking about it a lot. Don't even go there. You'll be glad you didn't.

Bad stuff on the Internet is just an example of stuff that's all around you that just isn't any good for you. Probably the best way to avoid all that bad stuff is to obey your parents' rules. If you follow their guidelines you'll miss out on about 90% of the bad stuff out there.

Unfortunately Eddie learned this lesson the hard way. One night he decided to disobey his mom, sneak out, and . . . well let's just say this mistake involved a Doberman, $300 in damages, and a security guard named Earl. Eddie's still paying that one off.

There's good news and there's bad news regarding this whole temptation thing. The bad news is it won't ever go away. Just ask somebody—your mom, dad, or your 85-year-old neighbor—they'll all tell you that as long as you're living on this earth, you'll face temptation. Even Jesus was tempted.

Did you know that Jesus met the devil face-to-face? The devil tempted him and tried to trick Jesus into doing something wrong. But in the final stand-off, guess who blinked? That's right, the old tempter himself was defeated. Check it out in Matthew 4:1-11.

The good news is you can beat temptation just like Jesus did! Now don't go around looking for tempting situations—that doesn't honor God—but when they find you (and they will), call on Jesus. He'll do the fighting for you. It's kind of like a tag-team wrestling match. Isn't it cool that your tag-team partner is God?

BOTTOM LINE

The one cool thing about facing temptation is that it gives you a chance to choose the right thing. God doesn't ever tempt us or cause us to do wrong (check it out in James 1:13), but he does allow us to take a kind of "pop quiz." Every time you say no to doing the wrong thing, you're saying yes to God. So be excited. This is a great chance to grow into maturity and to get closer to your heavenly Dad.

BOTTOM BOTTOM LINE

You've got to know by now that you're responsible for making good choices, but sometimes bad things or temptations just come upon you. When they do, just let Jesus know you need his help. Pray something like this:

Dear Lord, help! This thing is really hard for me to beat.
Will you give me the strength and power to
get through it without messing up?
Lord, help me tag—team with you.
Thanks. Amen.

Apparently Jason missed the memo
about the maid moving to Alaska.

CHAPTER 2:
Getting the
work done

He who is faithful in what is least is faithful also in much.
Luke 16:10

WORK...WHAT WORK?

One of your parents' expectations for you while you're home alone is probably to get your work done. Homework, cleaning your room, and chores are among the usual suspects. Here are some tips for getting it all done and still having time for a game of hoops.

One way to make sure you get all the stuff done is to make a list of the things you need to do that day, such as studying for the quiz in English, washing the dog, and putting your laundry away. Check stuff off as you do it. Kind of like this:

Stuff to do:
☑ math homework
☑ feed dog
☐ vacuum
☐ wash camel
☐ english quiz
☐ laundry

DO YOUR HOMEWORK.
(OR HOW TO LEARN AS MUCH AS YOU CAN BEFORE DINNER)

There's a little-known truth about teachers: each of them likes to assign homework as if his were the only class you take. But that's OK. You've got this book so you can defeat the Homework Monster.

Socrates said "Know Thyself." No wonder he made the big bucks as a sage and philosopher! But you know, old Sock had a point. One of the best ways to get ahead (especially in this whole homework deal) is to know what you're like.

Is it hard for you to relax until your homework's done? Do you need to unwind a little before you do anything? Do you get your assignments done right away or do you procrastinate?

There are no right or wrong answers to these questions, but it's really helpful to know yourself as you plan your afternoon. As you get to know your personality, your homework regimen will improve.

Take the following quiz to see where you fall on the homework scale:

Homework quiz

1. When I get home I like to

   a. eat something.

   b. get right to my homework so I can relax afterwards.

   c. play a little to unwind.

   d. relax first, homework later.

Hey, this is a great way to figure out how you work. If you work better after you've rested for awhile, definitely do that. If you're better off hitting the books right after you get home, then plan to do that. The important thing is to do what works for you.

2. My hardest subject this year is

   a. math.

   b. English.

   c. science.

   d. music.

   e. all of the above.

Leading researchers (OK it was just Flav, but it does make sense) say that you should do your hardest homework first, while your brain is freshest.

3. When it comes to homework, I

    a. just can't wait to do it. You just can't learn enough in one day, I always say.

    b. have to drag myself into doing it.

    c. don't even bother with it. I hate it.

    d. always seem to have something better to do, like watering my cactus garden.

Boy, that's a hard one. If you answered either c. or d. then you may need some pointers. Ask yourself, why is this so hard for me? Is it because I don't understand the stuff? Am I just not interested? Should I ask for help from my mom or dad? Am I getting discouraged because I seem to be falling behind in my studies and it's looking hopeless?

The first thing you should do is talk to your parents. Let them know what's going on. And talk to your teachers. Let them know what's bothering you. Don't go through this alone. They really do want to help you.

MORE GOOD TIPS FOR STUDYING

1. Do your homework at the same time every day if you can. If you start studying at 3:00 every day, it's like your body's saying, "Wow, it's 3:00, it must be time to study. Hey, brain, wake up!"

2. It's also a good idea to study at the same place each day. It doesn't really matter where: desk, floor, bed. One girl we know always does her math in the bathroom. But try to be consistent. Again your brain says, "Wow, we're at the desk, must be time to do homework."

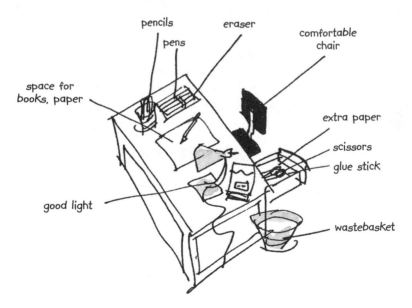

pencils

pens

eraser

comfortable chair

space for books, paper

extra paper

scissors

glue stick

good light

wastebasket

3. Try to have your desk—or wherever you'll be doing your homework—set up so that everything you need is within your reach. Think about it. You're on a roll, writing your pirate story for English. It's going great, when all of a sudden you misspell something. Yikes! You need an eraser! So now you have to get up, go through everything in your room, and check the whole house, all in search of a simple eraser! By the time you find it, you've spent fifteen minutes and completely gotten out of the mood to talk about pirates. So get all your stuff together—pens, pencils, erasers, plenty of paper and all the books you're going to need. Then you'll be able to study with no interruptions.

> ✳ Got an essay due? Can't think of what to write? Don't just stare at the blank page. Start writing! You can always go back and fix it later.

CLEAN YOUR ROOM

One of your after-school chores may be to clean your room. Here are some ideas for accomplishing this dreaded task.

As tempting as it is to drop your clothes on the floor, take 15 to 30 seconds to hang up the things you're going to wear again and stuff the dirty things in a laundry bag. That way they'll be available (and clean!) the next time you need them.

Here are some cool ideas for dealing with dirty clothes.

1. Put a basketball hoop in your room with a basket underneath it. See how many three-pointers you can make with your dirty clothes.

2. Get a duffel bag from the army surplus store and stick your dirty stuff in there. March into the laundry room and shout "Yes sir!" and "No sir!" every time you deliver it.

3. Make a life-size replica of yourself using your dirty clothes. Create an outfit then stuff the extra dirty things inside to fill it out. Use a pillow for the head. Carry yourself into the laundry area and drop yourself on the floor.

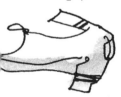

GET ORGANIZED!

What's easier than cleaning up? Keeping things clean and put away in the first place. If you get kind of organized, keeping things clean gets a lot easier.

Organizational tips
by Kacey Joiner

Do you ever spend hours looking for a lost CD or book from school? Have you ever accused someone of stealing something from you only to find it later in your room under a pile of stuff? Is it often difficult to find or identify the floor in your room?

If you answered yes to these questions, you might need some help in the organization department. I used to be so disorganized that I was late everywhere I went because I could never find my shoes. But I've reformed and now I can share these helpful hints with you to help keep your act together, too.

1. Keep a plastic box near your bed where you can put stuff you're going to need the next day. Use it to hold gym clothes, shoes, permission slips, assignments—you know, things like that. Then when you're running late the next morning you won't spend twenty extra minutes looking for that mising number 2 pencil.

2. Clean out your backpack at least a couple times a month. Get rid of papers and old stuff you don't need. That will help you find things more easily and give your back a break by lightening the load.

3. Get a bulletin board. Pin important papers up there—things like team practice schedules, dates for big assignments, important phone numbers, and the school calendar. That way you'll always know where those things can be found.

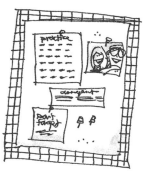

There are endless lists and guides to help you get organized, but hopefully the few ideas in this section will make your life a lot easier and give you more time for the truly important things like eating and doing nothing. Try some of these tips or make up some of your own.

The Son of Man did not come to be served, but to serve.
Matthew 20:28

HOW COME I DO ALL THE WORK? HOUSEHOLD CHORES

In order for your family to keep running, everybody's got to chip in and do her part. If you're like most kids, though, somehow your parents have managed to give you all the hard stuff to do around the house while your brother or sister hardly have to do anything. What's with that? Even if that's the case, you can't help what they do, so it's up to you to do the stuff you need to do.

TRASH

When you walk into the kitchen, do the whiff test. Do things smell fresh like a sweet-smelling spring breeze? Cool. Or does the place smell like someone stuffed six-week-old pizzas, a pair of gym socks, and a sock-eyed salmon in the oven and left it at 250 degrees for three days?

If that's the case, then it could just be time to do your parents (and your whole neighborhood) a favor and TAKE OUT THE TRASH! If you want to earn extra brownie points, put a clean trash bag in the container. Your mom—and the Environmental Protection Agency—will thank you for it.

RECYCLE

If your town has a recycling service, then instead of throwing stuff like paper, bottles, and cans away, recycle them! Newspapers and old school papers can go in, too.

Recycle

DISH DUTY

This chore is pretty boring, but it's got to be done. Try to make it more interesting by pretending you run a tacky diner in a Texas border town and you're cleaning up after the dinner rush. Or imagine that you've been captured by Martians and they're making you wash all the meteor gunk off all the smaller saucers while they return to the mother ship.

Even if the dishes aren't your responsibility, here's a good rule to use around the kitchen: if you dirty it, clean it up. In other words, if you use a glass or plate, either wash it or rinse it off and put it in the dishwasher when you're done with it. It's what you'd want someone to do for you, isn't it?

PETS

You love your dog. Or cat. Or fish. Or gerbil. Your pet loves you. But unlike your pets, you have a chance to express your love in tangible ways such as feeding them and giving them attention. Make sure they've always got food and water and take a few minutes to play with them (maybe not your fish). Pets need that kind of love.

In fact, Proverbs says that a righteous person gives his animals good care. So don't you want to be righteous and take care of Fido or Fishy? Sure you do.

LAUNDRY

In some families, kids help with the laundry. If that's the case with you, make sure you do it right. Don't fill the washing machine too full of clothes and make sure you remember the detergent. The manufacturer usually prints instructions on the lid of the machine. READ THEM! Have your mom show you which setting to put the washer on and then let 'er spin.

While the stuff is washing, go fix a snack or do some homework. Then do the same thing while the clothes are in the dryer. If you want to win the "Kid-of-the-Year" award, actually fold the clean clothes and lay them on their owner's bed. No one will believe it—guaranteed. They'll think you're up to something.

Housework: How I Do It
By Kacey Joiner

Hi. When they asked me to write this column on housework, I was a little bit surprised because I HATE HOUSEWORK!!! Whew. I'm glad I got that out.

My chores after school are picking up the house and vacuuming. Now, picking up doesn't mean stuffing everything in a closet so it's out of sight. Boy, did I learn that the hard way. Once my great-aunt Carlyle accidentally opened my closet door and whooosh! It took us three hours to dig her out.

Since I hate it so much, I try to do the housework as quick and easy as possible. Our vacuum cleaner is kept in the front closet, so I start at the room farthest away and work my way back so when I'm all done, I just put it away. Make sure you get every place on the floor and remember to ask your mom or dad to change the bag every now and again. That can be messy.

As for dusting, just get a clean cloth and, you know, dust! Make sure you do a thorough job. It's a good idea to dust before you vacuum. That way anything you get on the floor will be picked up, too.

And when your parents come home, feel free to take them on a tour of your work. That's what I do. Happy cleaning!

◈ REALITY CHECK

OK, let's talk honestly. Nobody really likes doing chores—especially if you feel like you're doing way more than everybody else. But look at it this way, doing things for others and doing them well is a great opportunity to become more like Jesus.

Philippians 2:5-8 says that Jesus laid down all his privileges as King of the Universe and came here to earth to become a servant. That's pretty amazing isn't it? And then he gave up his life for us! So if Jesus did all that for us, we can certainly manage to take out some trash occasionally. And there's something that happens to us when we're serving people—whether it's going on a missionary trip or feeding the cat—we start to change because God's Spirit is working inside of us.

BOTTOM LINE

Here's a secret to doing stuff well: ask God to help you do it. Just say, "Lord, if I have to wash one more dish or do one more load of laundry, I think I may just lose it. And that wouldn't be good. So help me to do this. Give me strength for what you're asking me to do, and help me to have a good attitude. Amen."

BOTTOM BOTTOM LINE

If you really think the way the chores are handed out is unfair, go to your parents and calmly discuss it with them. Trade off on chores or trade weeks. As long as the chores get done, your parents will be happy. And when they're happy, you'll be happy.

"And whatever you do in word or deed,
do all in the name of the Lord Jesus,
giving thanks to God the Father through him."
Colossians 3:17

Brandon is a firm believer
in adding variety to his diet.

CHAPTER 3:
Snacktime!

Your body is the temple of the
Holy Spirit who is in you. 1 Corinthians 6:19

THERE'S NOTHING TO EAT!

Do you ever feel this way? You look in the fridge—
nothing! The pantry—nada! And it's the middle of
the afternoon. A person could starve by the time
anybody got home!

Don't worry, because we've come up with more than
fifteen good-tasting, easy and (almost) healthy recipes
for you to enjoy while you're waiting for dinner. By the
way, these are just some ideas to get you started. If you
think of some others, jot them down. Be creative.
The sky (and your taste buds) is the limit.

WHY EAT RIGHT?

If you're like 99.9% of all kids, eating healthy isn't high on your list of priorities. Your motto is, "If it tastes good, eat it." But there really are some benefits to eating stuff that's good for you.

1. Eating right gives you more energy. Have you ever noticed how sluggish you feel when you've eaten a lot of sweets? It's like the sugar gets you going right away, but about twenty minutes later you feel much more tired than you did before.

Instead of sugar, try eating a protein and a carbohydrate together (such as peanut butter on wheat bread). That's going to give you the right kind of energy.

2. If you're between the ages of zero and 21, your body is growing. You want to feed it right so it'll grow and be strong. Your body needs well-balanced nutrition including a variety of vitamins each day. And guess what? That candy bar or soft drink you're considering doesn't have many in it. Check out the nutritional info on the wrapper or can.

3. One word—cavities.

4. The Bible says that our bodies are the temple of God's Spirit. That means he lives inside of us. So it seems like he'd like us to take care of our bodies. That doesn't mean you can't have candy, cupcakes, and ice cream occasionally, but it's just not good to make them your steady diet.

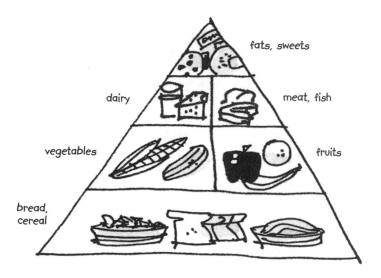

Here's that famous food pyramid you see on cereal boxes and bread wrappers. Basically what it means is you should eat more of the stuff towards the bottom, such as breads and cereals, fruits and vegetables and less of the stuff on top, such as candy and sweets. It's pretty simple, really.

Flav's "No Cooking" Selections

Since Flav isn't allowed to get near the microwave after the cheese and toaster pastry incident, he's come up with the following delicious ideas.

Mini-sandwiches

Take some sliced salami and cheese and layer them on top of round butter crackers or wheat crackers.

Or how about getting a can of that processed cheese and making faces on some toasted English muffins? You can use olive or radish slices for eyes and a nose. Do the mouth and hair with the cheese.

Do-it-yourself deli sandwich

Get some sliced turkey, ham, or roast beef; add some thousand island dressing, tomato slices, lettuce, and sliced pickle on rye bread. Have some potato or macaroni salad or corn chips on the side.

Yogurt sundaes

Have your mom get some of those small yogurts at the store—you know, peach, vanilla, lemon, strawberry. Grab one out of the fridge, open it up and add some cereal, granola, or crushed vanilla cookies or graham crackers for a smooth, crunchy treat.

Peanut Butter Extravaganza
by Eddie Piel

Ever since I was a kid, I've loved peanut butter. I have it on everything—toast, bananas, cupcakes, and even fried chicken. Mmmm. Here are some ideas on how to be creative with nature's perfect food. Why not go wild and try some of these combinations?
Peanut butter and . . .

honey
apple or banana slices
dried peaches or apricots
raisins
celery sticks
toasted English muffins

Chocolate peanut butter dipping sauce

Spoon one cup of peanut butter into a bowl. Stir it around until it's smooth. Add two cups of cold milk a little bit at a time and stir until the peanut butter gets pretty smooth. Next, add a box of chocolate instant pudding mix and stir with a wire whisk for about two minutes until you've got a cool, chocolaty concoction. Put the bowl in the fridge for about 20-30 minutes. Get some vanilla wafers, graham cracker halves, marshmallows, apple slices, and/or bananas for dipping in the sauce. Delicious!

OK, so you've done the peanut butter thing and you're ready for something different. Kacey is about the only kid in her class that really tries to eat healthy. But despite what Eddie and Flav say, healthy doesn't mean it can't taste good. Here are a few of her suggestions.

Quick, Healthy Snacks
by Kacey Joiner

Dippy city
Put some ranch dressing in a small bowl. Dip carrot sticks, celery, broccoli, or cherry tomatoes in the dressing and enjoy! Also try some apple slices dipped in cheese or peanut butter, or dip baked chips in fat-free onion dip or ranch dressing.

Tuna surprise
In a bowl, mix one can of tuna (drained), a tablespoon of mayonnaise, and a teaspoon of pickle relish. If you like, add raisins or some chopped apple (or both). To make a sandwich, spread tuna mixture on some fresh wheat bread or make a salad by spooning this on a big piece of lettuce. Try some honey mustard dressing with it. Have carrot sticks on the side. Mmmmmm.

Blender Bliss

There's nothing better than a homemade milkshake, but there's nothing worse than using the blender without permission and some instruction. What a mess! Make sure it's OK for you to use the blender and have one of your parents show you the tricks, including making sure the lid is on tight! (Lots of kids make their milkshakes in plastic shakers with a lid. That way you don't even have to deal with the blender.)

Chocolate milkshake

In the blender or plastic shaker, mix one cup of milk, two scoops of chocolate or vanilla ice cream or frozen yogurt, and two tablespoons of chocolate syrup or powder. Blend for fifteen seconds (make sure the lid is on tight) or shake in the shaker for one minute. Pour into a glass and enjoy. You may want to be creative and add a banana or a tablespoon of peanut butter. Caramel is also awesome! Crushed sandwich cookies also taste great in a chocolate or vanilla shake.

Smoothies

These are sooo good and good for you. You can really be creative with smoothies. Cut up your favorite fruits—bananas, peaches, strawberries, boysenberries, raspberries—and put these and a cup of plain or vanilla yogurt into the blender or shaker. Add a cup of orange juice and blend or shake for fifteen seconds.

Sweet Treats

Pudding dirt cups

Make a box of instant pudding. Chocolate works best for this. After you whip it up, let the pudding stand for about five minutes.

Crush half of a sixteen-ounce package of chocolate sandwich cookies in a bowl. Add three cups of whipped topping to the crushed cookies, then gently mix with the pudding.

Place some more of the crushed cookies into the bottom of plastic cups (about a tablespoon in each cup). Add the pudding mixture until the cups are full. Keep in the refrigerator for about twenty minutes to chill, then enjoy. To make it really look cool, add some candy gummy worms coming out of the "dirt."

Strawberry shortcake

The easiest way to make strawberry shortcake is to get an already baked pound cake at the store (either frozen or fresh from the bakery). Cut a slice and put it on a plate. Wash and slice four or five strawberries, and put the slices onto the cake. Then add some whipped cream. Oh, so easy and so good!

Mud pie

Get four to six chocolate sandwich cookies and crush them up in a bowl. Add two scoops of coffee (or any flavor) ice cream on top of the cookies. Add two tablespoons of chocolate syrup over the whole thing and then add some whipped cream if you'd like. There you have it! Delicious, quick mud pie!

Cinnamon toast

It's easy to make up a yummy cinnamon powder to sprinkle on toast. In a small bowl combine a cup of white sugar with one tablespoon of cinnamon. Mix them thoroughly. Place in a plastic container or sugar bowl with a lid. When you want cinnamon toast, just make your toast, butter it, and while the butter's still hot, sprinkle the cinnamon sugar on top. Easy, simple, yummy.

Ice cream sandwiches

These are really good and totally easy. Take some ice cream out of the freezer for about fifteen minutes to let it soften up. Get two chocolate chip, coconut, or oatmeal raisin cookies and lay them on a plate. Smoosh a scoop of the ice cream on one of the cookies. Add the second cookie as a lid on top. Voila! You've got an easy, delicious treat. Don't forget to put the ice cream back in the fridge or your family will be drinking their dessert this evening.

Microwave Madness

If it's OK for you to use the microwave, there are some really hot snacks you can put together in a couple of minutes. Note: Never ever put metal (including aluminum foil) in the microwave!

Popcorn

Microwave popcorn is an easy and sort of healthy snack you can fix in about three minutes. Ask your mom to get several bags of different flavors. Follow the directions on the bag and be careful when you pull it out. It'll be really hot. And never leave the room while the popcorn's in the microwave—it could catch on fire. And that would not be good.

Indoor s'mores

You've probably had s'mores when you went camping or with your scout troop. But you can fix these s'mores anytime, rain or shine. Put a piece of chocolate bar and a marshmallow on a square of graham cracker. Place on a microwave-safe plate in the microwave and set on high for ten seconds. (Any longer and the marshmallow will blow up like a balloon.) When it's done, bring it out (Careful—it'll be HOT!) and put another graham cracker on top to make a sandwich. Squish down and enjoy. Watch out—these can be addictive.

Mini-pizzas

Put two English muffins on a microwave-safe plate. Top them both with some grated cheese, a tablespoon of pizza or spaghetti sauce and a few small slices of pepperoni. Put in the microwave on high for one minute and fifteen seconds. Be careful when you bring them out, they'll be HOT! Let them cool down for about five minutes and enjoy. You may get creative and add a tomato slice, onions, even broccoli or some canned tuna.

Vamanos amigos burritos

Put a corn or whole wheat tortilla on a paper towel. Place a slice of cheese or some shredded cheese on top. Add some refried beans (these come in a can) and place in the microwave for 30-60 seconds, depending on your microwave. When the cheese starts to melt it's ready. Add diced tomatoes or salsa. Add lettuce and sour cream if you want to be fancy. This is great and will really fill you up (unless you're Todd or Eddie).

Nachos and salsa

These are even easier than the burritos. Put some tortilla chips on a microwave-safe plate. Lay some strips of cheddar or jack cheese on top of them. (Or you can pour some of that processed cheese on them.) Place in the microwave for fifteen seconds. Take them out, let them cool for about a minute, then pour on some salsa and maybe some sour cream. Enjoy.

 REALITY CHECK

The way God made our bodies is totally awesome. Think about it. All the things going on inside of us are nourished and built up by the foods we eat. God could have made us like plants—just stand in the sun, get wet occasionally, and grow. But instead, he designed us to live on the protein, fruits, and vegetables that he provides for us each day. Even though some of these may not be your favorites (like cauliflower and liver), each one is necessary for proper growth and strength.

Stuff you enjoy eating, like hamburgers and ice cream, are gifts from God, too. It's OK to eat those some of the time, but it's important to eat stuff that's good for you, too. That way you'll be building up your body and building up your spirit as well. God says that your body is the temple (or dwelling place) of his Holy Spirit, so you definitely want to take good care of it. When you choose to do the right thing by eating healthy foods, you're learning to honor God with your body.

BOTTOM LINE

When you learn to discipline yourself in the area of eating, you're telling your body who's boss. After all, who knows better what's good for you, you or your stomach? Read what Paul says in I Corinthians 9:27 about learning to control your body.

Why not write down some of your own ideas for cool (or hot) after-school snacks. Be creative, but make sure you always clean up your mess!

You Are Here

Never one to get bored,
Ashley builds famous landmarks
out of pretzels and canned frosting. . .

CHAPTER 4:
I'm bored!

For he is our God, and we are the people of his pasture, and the sheep of his hand. Psalm 95:7

THERE'S NOTHIN' TO DO!

OK, you've finished your homework, had a snack, fed the dog, and put all your stuff away. Now what? What are you going to do for two and a half hours?

If you're like a lot of kids, you could plunk down in front of the TV and watch a couple of hours of those talk shows where people are yelling at one another about whether or not they really did see the UFO. Or you could play video games or get on the Internet. The thing is, you're not like most kids. You're unique. Creative. Just a little bit wacky. So why not use this time to do something really different?

Think about the things you really enjoy. Why not get as good as you can at them, then use them to bless other people? Here are some suggestions.

1. If you like writing or drama, write a story or play that shows how God loves us and wants to be involved in our lives. See if one of the Sunday school classes at your church will act it out.

2. If you like animals, offer to watch someone's pet, either at your house or his, while he's away on vacation.

3. Do you like to draw? Make a card or comic strip for a neighbor or friend—maybe even your teacher.

STILL DON'T KNOW
WHAT TO DO?

On the following pages, you're going to find the best list of amazing stuff to do if you're bored. Try some of these, or use them as a springboard for your own ideas. You may even decide to try one of these each day for the next 101 days (that's a little over three months).

101 Amazing Things To Do
When You're Bored

1. Use the video camera to record commercials for made-up products.
2. Teach the cat how to fetch.
3. Set up a miniature golf course inside your house.
4. Draw a comic strip with yourself as the star.
5. Dust.
6. Make up a new dance step to some cool music.
7. Play volleyball against an outside wall.
8. Write letters to a pen pal.
9. Make your own pop-up book.
10. Read half of a novel, then write your own ending.
11. Using your tape recorder, make a radio show.
12. Put your photos and memories together in a scrapbook.
13. Practice doing push-ups.

14. Organize and label all your videotapes or DVD's.

15. Make your own crossword puzzle. Use a dictionary.

16. Use magazine clippings to make a collage that describes who you are.

17. Go lawn bowling: roll a beach ball at two-liter bottles.

18. Play some fast music and make up an aerobics routine.

19. Get a French book and learn a new word every day.

20. Do the same thing with Spanish.

21. Find out if there's a missionary from your church in some foreign country and write him or her a letter.

22. Vacuum the house.

23. Make up your own language.

24. Get some gel and a hair dryer and create outrageous new do's for yourself.

25. Make a calendar.

26. Make a list of all the cool things about yourself.

27. Make a list of the things you'd like God to help you change.

28. Read a chapter from the Gospel of John every day.

29. Memorize a Scripture verse.

30. Tear a page from one of your magazines and glue it to cardboard. Then cut it up and make a puzzle.

31. Practice doing crunches or sit-ups.

32. Make a list of things you'd do with one million dollars.

33. Write your own neighborhood newspaper.

34. Read a children's story into a tape recorder and give the tape to a child you know.

35. Shoot 25 free throws in a row. If you miss one, start over.

36. Take the trash out.

37. Rewrite the words to your favorite song.

38. Learn how to stand on your head by leaning against a wall. Take your shoes off first.

39. Design your dream house. Don't forget the basketball court and ice cream parlor.

40. Make a list of people you know—kids and adults—and pray for one person each day.

41. Organize your closet.

42. And your drawers!

43. Learn how to play the guitar or ukulele.

44. Run in place for one minute each day this week. Add one minute per week until you can go ten minutes without stopping.

45. Design a magazine ad for a product you really like.

46. Draw your own hieroglyphics.

47. Find some toys you had when you were younger and play with them (you know you want to).

48. Write your own stand-up comedy routine.

49. Clean out your closet and give your old things to a charity.

50. Make up riddles.

51. Write limericks. You know, poems like this:

> To spend some time after school
> A kid showed he wasn't a fool,
> He'd write all these poems
> To people he'd show 'em
> And soon they all saw he was cool.

(You know you can do better than this!)

52. Use modeling clay to sculpt a figure of yourself.

53. Play a game.

54. Roll up socks in a ball and have a sock war with your brother or sister. (Better take this war outside!)

55. Create your own personal slogan.

56. Read a chapter from the *Chronicles of Narnia* series.

57. Measure to see how tall you are.

58. Do a jigsaw puzzle.

59. Paint a watercolor picture.

60. Create your own city, either on paper or out of modeling clay.

61. Write a note to a teacher that you really appreciate. Put it on his or her desk tomorrow.

62. Design the ultimate paper airplane.

63. Make your own stickers out of contact paper.

64. Write your own joke book.

65. Write out some of your favorite Scripture verses and put them under everybody's pillows.

66. Set up an obstacle course in your yard. Time how fast it takes everyone to get through it.

67. Draw what it must have looked like inside Noah's ark.

68. Measure today's rainfall with either a wide-mouthed jar or an empty tuna can.

69. Put together a show to perform at dinner tonight.

70. Make a coin jar. Put your loose change into it every day. Then give the money to a missionary.

71. Make a bird feeder by covering a pinecone with peanut butter and rolling it in birdseed.

72. Make up your football, basketball, or baseball dream team.

73. Cast your own movie with your Hollywood Dream Team.

74. Get your most recent school picture and draw a different body under it.

75. Hide a treat, then play "you're getting warmer" until someone finds it.

76. Practice soccer moves with a balloon.

77. Get two of today's newspapers and play "find the article" with a friend. You find an article, photo, or cartoon, tell your friend what it is and see how long it takes to find it.

78. Speak everything in Pig Latin. (Ig-pay Atin-Lay)

79. Make coupons for your parents—like "One free back rub" or "One free lunch out, my treat."

80. Try your hand at knitting, crochet, or cross-stitch.

81. Get a map of the world and figure out a route you'd like to take to go around it.

82. Rearrange the furniture, then blindfold someone and talk that person through the room so that he doesn't bump into anything. You can't touch him, you can only say, "Straight ahead, turn left" and stuff like that.

83. Measure to see how tall you are. See if you've grown since number 57.

84. Teach the dog a trick.

85. Make a menu of your favorite meal.

86. Make postcards and send them to your friends.

87. Put your clothes on backwards and when your mom gets home, back into the room.

88. Get a book on quilting and try sewing a quilt block.

89. Make a weekly calendar with stuff to do.

90. Shoot three-pointers using rolled-up socks and a wastebasket.

91. When your dad (or mom) gets home greet him with his slippers and a warm washcloth for his face.

92. Research and celebrate lesser-known holidays, like Boxing Day and National Donut Day.

93. Make up a major corporation of which you're the president. Figure out how your company makes and sells a product.

94. Write your autobiography.

95. Dream about your perfect vacation.

96. Figure out new, hip names for all the planets.

97. Create a country. Draw a map of its resources, including a large amusement park and beach.

98. Start a prayer journal.

99. Invent something that needs to be invented.

100. Study Morse code, then send a message to your friend at night with a flashlight. (Make sure he or she knows how to decipher it).

101. Write your own TV theme song.

✦ REALITY CHECK

Whew! That's one big list! Hopefully you found something (or a lot of things) in there you can do when you're bored.

But you know sometimes it's OK to be still and quiet for awhile. With TV, videos, computers, telephones, CD players, and radios all around, when was the last time you were just quiet? Of course there's nothing wrong with being busy and active, but sometimes when you're too busy, you may miss something that God's trying to tell you.

If you're going 100 miles an hour through every day, what are the chances you're going to be still long enough to hear from the Lord? Try being still every so often. Read a little bit from your Bible. Ask God to speak to you. He will. Oh, it probably won't be a voice you can hear out loud, but in your heart you may get a sense of something he wants to tell you like how much he loves you. Listen. He'll speak to you.

Be still, and know that I am God.
Psalm 46:10

BOTTOM LINE

Take a moment and write down a couple of things.
First, write down what you think God may be
saying to you.

Write some of the ways you can use your gifts and
talents to bless others. What are some of the things you
like to do? How can God use those things
to help other people?

You
Are
Here

In an attempt to add realism
to the family fire drills,
Brandon started holding them
at 3 a.m. . . .

CHAPTER 5:
Safety & handling emergencies

The fear of man brings a snare, but whoever trusts in the Lord shall be safe. Proverbs 29:25

DON'T WORRY

It's no fun to worry about all the things that could go wrong while you're home alone. So our advice is—don't. Worry, that is. Now it's OK to figure out ways to handle little problems that come up, and it's important that you and your parents are on the same wavelength as far as safety. But to sit and worry about it is pretty useless. Make sure you tell your mom or dad about the things that are bothering you and figure out ways to take care of them.

The most important thing to do is realize that God is with you. You know, the Lord. Jesus. The battle of Jericho and David's battle against Goliath are just two examples from the Bible that show God's ability to handle bad situations. You can rest in the confidence that God's never going to leave you or forget about you. Just tell him when you're nervous. Or worried. Or just kind of lonesome. He wants to help you. He wants you to learn to trust him no matter what you're facing.

A good way to remember to take safety steps is to follow a routine. This example takes care of general safety stuff.

1. Come in, hang up the keys.

2. Close and lock the door.

3. Put your school stuff in your room.

4. Call Mom or Dad (or a neighbor) to let them know you're home.

✳ You and your parents may ask your neighbors if they can be a "safe house" for you. That means you can go there or call them in case of an emergency.

Here's a helpful little quiz to help you figure out the right, safe responses to things that could come up.

KNOCK, KNOCK

OK, let's say you're home alone and a stranger comes to the door. It's an adult who's dressed nice and is very friendly. Should you

a) swing the door open and welcome the person in with open arms.

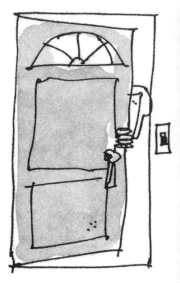

b) don't open the door, but yell loudly, "I can't come out, I'm in the bathtub!"

c) keep the door closed, but talk to the person through it.

d) ignore the person altogether.

If you answered d, you chose the best thing to do. Just don't answer the door at all. Always make sure it's locked and don't open it for anyone you don't know: salespeople, people handing out flyers, people who say they lost their dog. No one.

UNWANTED COMPANY

You think you hear someone breaking into the house, or when you arrive, you can tell that somebody's been there. How should you handle that?

a) Try to remember how all those action heroes—use martial arts.

b) Get out of the house and go to your "safe house" to call your parents or the police.

c) Check to make sure that your football card collection is still safe.

d) Go out to the street and break into the intruder's car.

Obviously the only sane answer here is b. The most important thing to do in this situation is get out of there. Go to your safe house and tell your neighbor what's going on. If there is someone in your house, you'll need to call 911. Then call your parents at work. Then stay put. Wait until the police get there and they make sure it's safe.

PLAYING TELEPHONE

What if someone keeps calling and
either hangs up or says bad stuff to
you? What should you do?

a) Don't answer the phone.
Let the answering
machine get it.

b) Pick up the phone and say
"Hello, America's Most Wanted,
are we looking for you?"

c) As soon as you know it's the mystery caller,
don't speak, just hang up.

d) Start asking questions like "Who are you?
Does your mommy know you're using the phone?"

The best answer is a. If you're going to be staying home alone, your family should really think about getting caller ID and/or an answering machine. That way, you don't have to answer the phone when you're by yourself unless you know it's your mom or dad.

But if you don't have caller ID you might work out a secret code with your parents. Have them call, let the phone ring once, and then hang up. Then have them call again right away. This time you'll know it's them and you can pick it up. Easy.

※ Your phone can play a very important role in your family's safety plan. Keep a complete, up-to-date list of emergency numbers next to or printed on every phone in the house.

PET SAFETY

When you're home alone, you're responsible for the safety of your pet, too. The safest place for your pets is in the house with you or in the backyard with the gate closed. Be smart and careful to make sure Fido doesn't get out!

What do you do if your dog does get out when you're home alone? Do you go and search for him? Probably not. You may call  an adult friend on your street and tell them what happened. Maybe they can go look for the pooch. But if you're not supposed to leave the house, you shouldn't do it for any reason.

GUN SAFETY

What should you do if you find a gun in your house or one of your friends is playing with a gun? This is a real possibility, so here's a simple rule to follow: Get out of there!

If you find a gun in the house, leave it alone and get out of there! Don't pick it up. Don't handle it. Don't even touch it. Just get out of there!

And if some kid you're hanging out with (no matter where you are) starts waving a gun around . . . you got it . . . get out of there!

Don't ask questions. Don't check it out. Don't be cool. Just leave. And if you can, let an adult know about the gun and let him handle the situation. That's the best idea yet.

YOUR SUPERHERO SELF: KEEPING COOL IN AN EMERGENCY

Even if you follow all the safety rules mentioned above, and all the rules your parents give you, sometimes you find yourself with an emergency on your hands anyway. Nobody likes to think of an emergency, and odds are you'll go through this whole after-school thing with nothing ever happening. Even so, it's good to know what to do just in case.

The first thing to do is pray. Remember God? He's still with you—emergency or not. So be sure to talk to him right away. Pausing to ask him to help you not only will calm you down, but also will help you deal with the situation much better.

Your Telephone:
The Best Tool in an Emergency or When and How to Call 911

1. Tell what kind of emergency it is (for example: fire, injury, break-in).

2. Stay on the line, follow the operator's instructions.

3. Tell them the address and the closest cross-streets.

NEVER call 911 as a joke.

ACCIDENTS AND FIRST AID

Now that you're going to be home alone, you should learn some simple first aid to use around the house. That's a good topic to discuss with your parents. Why not get a good book on household first aid and have it on hand as a reference? Your favorite bookstore or the library should have one. Read through it. Get familiar with some of the ways you can learn to take care of minor emergencies.

Some communities offer first aid classes for kids through the local hospital, library, or YMCA. You may want to check those out, too. Give these places a call to see what they teach. It'll probably make you feel a lot more confident and comfortable if you know how to take care of this kind of stuff when you're on your own.

FIRST AID KIT

Every home (especially with kids) should have a
well-stocked first aid kit. Here are some must-have
items that should be in there:

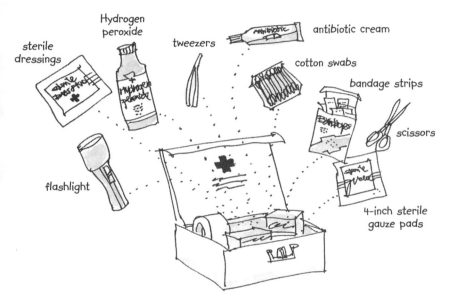

sterile dressings

Hydrogen peroxide

tweezers

antibiotic cream

cotton swabs

bandage strips

scissors

flashlight

4-inch sterile gauze pads

DO I SMELL SMOKE?

It's afternoon or early evening and suddenly you start to smell smoke. The smoke detector goes off. What should you do?

a) Get the garden hose and put out the fire.

b) Run from room to room yelling "Fire! Fire!" (This is particularly effective if you're all by yourself.)

c) Get out of the house as fast as you can and go to a neighbor's. Call 911.

d) Get out the marshmallows.

If you answered c on this one, you're amazing! The absolute best thing to do if you suspect a fire is get out of the house! Go over to a neighbor's (or your safe house) and call 911. Tell them exactly where the fire is, your address, and a cross-street. Then stay where you are.

Fire Safety 101
by Eddie Piel

Hi there! Here are a few fire safety tips that my mom and I stick to ever since our cat Fluffy started a fire by knocking over a lighted candle. No major damage was done (well, Fluffy singed his whiskers), but it made us think about a plan. These tips have kept us safe, and if you follow them you will be safe, too.

1. Make sure your smoke alarms are working. Check the batteries every six months.

2. Have a good fire extinguisher. Know where it is and how to use it.

3. Plan a spot where the family will meet in case of fire. That way you'll know if everybody's out and safe.

4. Have a fire drill to make sure everyone knows . . . you know, the drill.

NATURAL EMERGENCY

An earthquake, tornado, hurricane, forest fire,
or all of the above are heading for your neighborhood.
Should you:

a) get out the video camera for some great shots.

b) hide under a blanket.

c) follow the guidelines your family has already set up.

d) move to another neighborhood.

You should have picked c on this one. Nobody likes
to think about things like earthquakes or tornados,
but your family should have a plan just in case.
Talk to your parents about what you should do in
an emergency like that. Is there a neighbor's house
you could go to?

If this is a big emergency, it's a good idea for your
family to have a contact outside the area that can
be alerted in case the phone service is interrupted.
This contact could be an aunt or uncle in another state.
Figure out what you should do ahead of time, how to
do it, and then do it.

Wow! When you read all this stuff you could say to yourself, "Aaaauuugggghhhh! This is scary! I don't want to be home alone!" Calm down and take a deep breath. You don't have to feel nervous.

First of all, the safety info in this section is just good old common sense. Besides, the chances of any of this bad stuff happening are really slim. You'll probably never face any of these problems, but if you do face them, it's good to be prepared.

More importantly, you've got to remember that God's going to take care of you no matter what emergency may happen. All the way through his Word, God's saying stuff like, "I'll never leave you" and "Don't be afraid." He doesn't want you to go through life filled with fear because when it's all said and done he's the one who's going to take care of you.

PHONE NUMBERS YOU NEED

All right! This is the part where you get to write the book. We've given you a start, but feel free to add all the numbers you may need in an emergency, like the pizza place, the local video rental, and the nearest convenience store.

Remember if you are making an emergency call, the number is usually 911, but check the front of your phone book to make sure of the emergency number in your area.

Your name _____

Your address _____

_____

Cross-streets _____

_____

Fire emergency 911 or _____

Fire non-emergency _____

Police emergency 911 or _____

Police non-emergency _____

Medical emergency 911 or_____

Hospital emergency room _____

Ask-a-nurse _____

Poison control center _____

Doctor _____

Dentist _____

Veterinarian _____

Power company (in case of power failure)_____

Plumber _____

Mom work _____cell _____

Dad work _____cell _____

Other contact person _____

Neighbor _____

Neighbor _____

Schools _____

Church _____

Contact person outside of area _____

Other_____

Other_____

REALITY CHECK

Staying home by yourself is like so many other things you'll do in life. There will be good days and hard days. There will be days when everything goes great, there's plenty of good stuff in the fridge, and you don't have any homework. And then there will be other days when your little brother is driving you crazy, the dog ate the last two donuts, you can't understand the math homework, and your parents call to say they're running late.

But if you and your parents can talk together to figure out how to make this work for everybody, it's going to be a cool experience. Just remember these five helpful hints.

1. Talk! Let your parents know what's working and what isn't. If you don't say anything, they'll never know.

2. Follow the rules. Do what you need to be safe and helpful.

3. Be responsible for yourself. This home-alone thing is one of your first steps to growing up and becoming (dare we say it?) an adult.

4. Pray about everything—the good and the bad. God wants to hear how you're doing and what he can do to help.

5. And finally, have fun and enjoy this brand new adventure!

You
Are
Here

Cool books for preteens!

SURVIVING
MIDDLE SCHOOL
written by
Sandy Silverthorne
0-7847-1433-9

SURVIVING
When You're
HOME ALONE
written by
Sandy Silverthorne
0-7847-1434-7

SURVIVING
ZITS
written by
Sandy Silverthorne
0-7847-1435-5